The Feisty Old Woman Who Lived in the Cozy Cave

Written by Virginia King • Illustrated by Sarah Farman

Once there was a feisty woman who lived in a cozy cave.

She was small,
and she was ninety years old.
But she was fierce
when she needed to be!

In the forest
there lived a bear.
He was big.
He was brown.
He was angry.
He had no cozy cave to sleep in.

The bear crashed through the forest and stopped outside the cozy cave. He called to the feisty old woman, "I will come in
and sleep in your cozy cave!"

The feisty old woman
stood at the door.
"No you won't!" she yelled.
"She's too fierce for me," said the bear,
and off he went.

In the forest
there lived a bat.
He was furry.
He was black.
He was angry.
He had no cozy cave to hang in.

The bat flapped through the forest and stopped outside the cozy cave. He called to the feisty old woman, "I will come in
and hang in your cozy cave!"

The feisty old woman
stood at the door.
"No you won't!" she yelled.
"She's too fierce for me," said the bat,
and he flew away.

In the forest
there lived a dragon.
He was scaly.
He was purple.
He was angry.
He had no cozy cave to breathe fire in.

The dragon thundered through the forest and stopped outside the cozy cave. He called to the feisty old woman, "I will come in and breathe fire in your cozy cave!"

The feisty old woman
stood at the door.
"No you won't!" she yelled.
"She's too fierce for me," said the dragon,
and off he went.

The bear went to sleep in a hollow log.

The bat hung upside down from a tree.

The dragon breathed fire in the moonlight.

The feisty old woman
went to sleep in her cozy cave.